Motivation

Master The Power Of Motivation To Propel Yourself To Success

By Ace McCloud
Copyright © 2014

Disclaimer

The information provided in this book is designed to provide helpful information on the subjects discussed. This book is not meant to be used, nor should it be used, to diagnose or treat any medical condition. For diagnosis or treatment of any medical problem, consult your own physician. The publisher and author are not responsible for any specific health or allergy needs that may require medical supervision and are not liable for any damages or negative consequences from any treatment, action, application or preparation, to any person reading or following the information in this book. Any references included are provided for informational purposes only. Readers should be aware that any websites or links listed in this book may change.

Table of Contents

Introduction 6
Chapter 1: The Importance of Motivation 8
Chapter 2: Motivation and Self-Regulation 11
Chapter 3: Ten Great Motivational Techniques 13
Chapter 4: Motivation Killers 18
Chapter 5: Motivation Role Models 21
Chapter 6: Motivational Quotes 24
Conclusion 26
My Other Books and Audio Books 27

Be sure to check out my website for all my Books and Audio books.

www.AcesEbooks.com

Introduction

I want to thank you and congratulate you for buying the book, "Motivation: Master The Power Of Motivation To Propel Yourself To Success."

Do you ever wish that you were more motivated? Do you ever think that success would come much easier if you had that inner desire and drive to get important things done? Motivation is a powerful force that anybody can utilize to become much more successful, happy, fulfilled, and inspired. However, if you do not know how to effectively utilize the power that motivation gives you and its powerful effects, your chances of reaching your goals is greatly diminished.

Just by reading the introduction of this book, I can already tell that you desire to learn more about motivation and how to harness its power. I can also tell that you desire to learn, grow, and succeed in both your personal life and career because you're actively looking for helpful information. In this book you will discover how to do all of this and more.

Motivation is a huge factor in whether your life is everything you want it to be, or not. Motivation has taken people across countries, to the highest peaks of success, and it has helped people accomplish things that have never been done before. Motivation is often the mighty push that will get you to pursue and excel in your true passions at a truly professional level.

This book contains proven steps and strategies on how to better understand what motivation really is by breaking it down into simple, easy, and understandable pieces. You will learn how motivation inspires different people to act and how to harness its power for your own success. You will also learn how to understand motivation a little better so that you can grasp it and use it as best as you can to accomplish your goals and dreams. You will learn about self-regulation and how it relates to strengthening your ability to be motivated. You will also learn 10 great techniques for becoming and staying motivated in your daily life. After that, you will learn some things *not* to do if you want to keep your motivation in life strong and helpful techniques that you can practice at home. Finally, you will read about some famous people and how they used motivation to get where they are now. At the end of this book will be a section containing some of the best motivational quotes that you can refer to anytime, whenever you are feeling discouraged or lost.

Additionally, you will learn about the most common motivation killers and how to avoid them. Finally, you will hear about motivation from some of the most inspirational people in history. So wait no longer, start your journey towards a motivated and successful life now.

Chapter 1: The Importance of Motivation

Have you ever found yourself really, really thirsty? What did you do? Odds are you went into your kitchen or you stopped at a vending machine and got something to drink. Have you ever been tired of feeling broke? What did you do? You probably went out and looked for a new job or looked into furthering your education so that you could work in a different field. Whenever you have a problem, whether it be a minor or major one, your normal reaction is usually to do something about it.

Why does that happen? What causes you to get off the couch and pour a glass of water or open up your laptop and update your resume, among the other things that you do? The answer is motivation.

Motivation is the invisible force that initiates you to action towards your goals, dreams and desires. Your brain isn't just programmed to find a solution to a problem. You have to *want* to find a solution, no matter how big or small. The *want* in you is your motivation. Motivation is asking *why*. Why do I want/need to do something? This usually breaks down into avoiding pain or gaining pleasure. Most people will be highly motivated to drive good to avoid the pain caused by an accident or a ticket, and most people will try and be friends with people they get along with and trust for the pleasure this type of bond can bring. If you're not feeling compelled to reach your goal then you may want to find something else that motivates you or try using the techniques discussed in this book to help motivate yourself to get a particular goal accomplished.

Motivation is one of the main driving forces in your life. Whether or not you are motivated can determine how high up you go in your career, how much money you make, what kind of relationships you develop, how healthy your body is and much more. Those who report feeling more motivated tend to have higher activity levels, feel better about themselves and tend to get much better results in life than those who do not feel as motivated.

Where Does Motivation Come From?

The forces behind motivation are a combination of biological, social, emotional, and cognitive drives. In the world of biology, there are two different types of motivation: intrinsic and extrinsic. **Intrinsic motivation** represents the personal, internal reward that you get out of accomplishing something—for example, when you finish a puzzle, you don't usually get money or a trophy but you get a really good sense of accomplishment. **Extrinsic motivation** represents physical, tangible rewards that come with an achievement—for example, a degree for completing 4 years of college or a raise for achieving your work goals.

Since motivation is such a vast and complex topic, it has been studied by scientists, researchers, and psychologists for years. One of the most popular theories of motivation is the **theory of self-determination**, which states that you are self-motivated because you crave growth and fulfillment. Similar to intrinsic motivation, this theory suggests that you desire to learn different skills, feel a sense of belonging, and have control over your goals and actions. The theory further suggests that the desire to be self-motivated is a part of the desire to undergo personal growth.

Another common theory, the **arousal theory of motivation**, suggests that you become motivated to do things based on your level of arousal. For example, if you're sitting around at home and you're feeling bored, you may go for a walk or watch a movie to feel more excited. On the other hand, if you're feeling too excited or stressed out, you may take a relaxing bath or try some meditation to calm down.

The **humanistic theory of motivation** suggests that your motivations are prioritized based on the needs outlined by Maslow's Hierarchy of Needs. For example, this theory suggests that you will take action to fulfill hunger and thirst before do something to feel safe and secure, and so on, until you are motivated to feel self-actualization.

Emotions also play a big role in determining whether you are motivated to do something or not. Similar to the **instinct theory of motivation**, which suggests that motivation stems out of evolution, emotions can strongly influence your actions. If you want to love or feel loved, you will probably be motivated to get into the dating scene. If you want to feel happy or joyous, you will be more likely to pick up a hobby or make extra time to engage in an activity that you're good at. If you want to eliminate fear in your life, you will probably feel motivated to work on understanding and eliminating the underlying causes of your limiting beliefs.

Today, it seems that motivation is a combination of all of these theories. People are motivated for different reasons, but despite what those reasons are, motivation is still the process of taking action toward a goal.

What Does Motivation Consist Of?

No matter what kind of driving force is behind *your* motivation, it is important to know what motivation consists of. When it comes to being motivated, there are three common components: action, persistence, and intensity. When you take action, you actively do something to take one step forward toward your goal. For example, if you want to have a career in finance, you would take action by enrolling in a college with a good finance program and reading the best financial advice books.

When you are persistent, you continuously work toward your goal despite any challenges that come your way.

When you are intense in achieving your goal, you go above and beyond to really get there. You'll do whatever it takes, overcome any obstacles that come in your way, and you won't give up until you've achieved the end result.

Motivation is a very important aspect in life. It is what helps you accomplish your goals. When you are motivated to achieve your long-term goals, you can become very established in life. Motivation is what has made people famous. It is the reason why there have been medical breakthroughs, amazing books and movies, and excellent businesses and organizations. Anybody can master motivation and use it to do great things in life.

Chapter 2: Motivation and Self-Regulation

One of the most well-known theories of motivation is the self-regulation theory. When you practice self-regulation, you are putting forth the ability to regulate and control your actions, regardless of what your emotions are. In simpler terms, it's basically the act of picking yourself up and doing something, even if you are feeling lazy. So how does self-regulation play into motivation? Why is it so important?

The self-regulation theory of motivation states that a person can use self-regulation to help him or her achieve a long-term goal by mastering short-term goals. For example, if you can stop yourself from spending your money on little things, like an extra cup of coffee or a pack of cigarettes, you will eventually save up enough money in the long-term to buy yourself something nice, like a car.

It is very important to practice self-regulation. Without self-regulation, you can be prone to outbursts or impulsive behaviors. Hotheaded people can end up in jail because they act out of impulse and even normally calm people can lose friends due to emotional outbursts or money problems that come from uncontrolled spending habits. The good news is that self-regulation is relatively easy to learn.

Learning Self-Regulation

Since self-regulation is a driving factor in both your daily and long-term decisions, it is important to start practicing it as soon as possible. By simply learning about what it takes to practice self-regulation skills, you can start doing it right after you finish reading this book. Experts believe that there are four basic factors behind learning self-regulation.

The first thing you will need to do is set one or more **standards.** Without setting a standard, you will not know how you will need to change your current behavior. So, for example, if you are trying to stop spending money every day to try and save for something big, you will have to set your spending standards.

The second thing you will need to do is figure out how to **monitor** your behavior. If you do not keep track of your behavior, it can be hard to regulate your actions. Standards and monitoring go hand in hand because if you find that you're not reaching your standards through monitoring, you will have to reevaluate your situation. So, if you decide to monitor your spending by looking at your bank statements every day and you find that you're not meeting your standards, you will have to come up with a new strategy.

The third thing you will need to do is exert **willpower**. Your level of willpower is a huge factor in determining whether you will meet your long-term goal or not. This factor comes from inside of you—you will need to practice self-discipline so that you do not spend extra money, or do whatever it is that you're trying to change. If willpower is something that you need to work on, please check out my book Influence, Willpower, and Discipline.

Together, these three factors can help bring you to the fourth factor: **motivation.** When you want to achieve your long-term goal, setting standards, monitoring your progress, and exerting willpower can help you feel more motivated to reach the end result. You will already be in the habit of taking small, positive steps toward your end result.

How well you can handle and practice self-regulation is usually a predicting factor in how your life turns out. People who have poor self-regulation skills tend to abuse substances, have unwanted pregnancies, fail in relationships, get bad grades in school, and not hold jobs for long. For some people, it brings them into the life of crime. When a person experiences any of those situations, their chances of feeling motivated to succeed in life tend to go down. He or she tends to feel discouraged and accepts life "as it is." However, by knowing and understanding the theory of self-regulation, you can feel more motivated to accomplish great things in both the long-term and the short-term. Start by identifying a problem in your life that you would like to change—maybe your spending habits, maybe your exercise habits, it can be anything. Try to apply the self-regulation theory to help motivate yourself to success.

Chapter 3: Ten Great Motivational Techniques

One of the things about motivation is it doesn't just happen—it's something you need to constantly work at to keep it going for long periods of time. By making certain activities a habit, your motivation will naturally stay strong over weeks, months, or even years. This chapter will review 10 of the best techniques for becoming and staying motivated. You can try them all, in order, out of order, one at a time, or whatever works for you.

Top 10 Motivational Techniques

Develop Your Goals and Action Plan. To be motivated for anything, it is essential to set goals and know what you're going to do to reach them. Without goals, it is very hard to intelligently make a plan to steer your life in the direction desired. The first thing you can do to stay motivated in your life is to set goals and review them several times per day. A good and effective idea is to write your ideas down on paper and put them in a place where you can easily review them. When you write something down, you tend to retain it much better. Take a few minutes and write down some goals, if you don't have them already. A good strategy to utilize when making a goal is to make it seem easy. For example: I will easily workout four times per week or I will easily increase my income by two thousand dollars a month by the end of the year. At the bottom of your goal sheet, write in explicit detail why you want to accomplish your goals. Make this vision compelling and something that really excites you. Too many people make small goals that lack passion, don't be afraid to dream big and shoot for something truly incredible. Once you know what your goals are, the next thing to do is to develop an action plan.

Having goals is great but if you don't know how to work towards them, you will more than likely never reach them. Let's say that one of your goals is to start saving more money. You've got your goal—now think about your action plan. One idea could be to state that you will put aside $20 extra each week into a separate savings account. Another idea would be to list all of your expenses, and then to strategically go through them to see which ones can be reduced and which ones can be eliminated. Then be sure to read your goals and action plans at least once a day, if not more, to help keep you focused and feeling motivated towards accomplishing your goals. Any time you are not feeling motivated to keep up on your finances, be sure to refer back to your goals and action plans.

Figure Out Why Your Goals Matter. If you are not sure why you set the goals that you set for yourself, you may not feel as motivated to work toward them. By asking yourself *why* you want to reach each goal, you can be reminded of its true purpose. For example, your goal is to save money and you're going to put aside $20 each week...but why? Your answer might be that you want to buy a new car or take a nice vacation.

So, anytime you feel tempted to spend that extra $20 that you could be saving, think about *why* your goals matter. More than likely, that will help you stay motivated. One good idea to help yourself figure out why your goals matter is to write each one down and then write your thoughts on why you want to achieve them. You can use that opportunity to brainstorm your thoughts. You may end up coming up with several great reasons for each goal, which can push you even further to pursue your dreams.

Practice Accountability. By setting goals for yourself, you are greatly increasing your chances of achieving them. Some of your goals, especially your personal goals, may be private, meaning that only you know about them. To stay motivated in achieving them, you can practice accountability to get your end result.

There are several ways to practice accountability. If you don't mind other people knowing about your goals, you could hold yourself accountable on social media. If you prefer your goals to stay private, you could ask a close friend, relative or your partner to help you stay accountable. Many people call this an accountability partner. Set up plans where your accountability buddy contacts you once a week and asks how your goals are. By having somebody else hold you accountable, your chances of sticking to your goals can be higher.

For example, if you're trying to save money, ask somebody to call you up once a week and ask, "So how much have you saved so far?" If the answer doesn't meet the required goal, then there should be some sort of penalty for failure. This penalty should keep you motivated to get things done the right way during the week.

Eliminate Negativity. Negativity is a horrible emotion that generally serves no good purpose. Negativity is often a huge factor in why people become unmotivated. When you constantly hear negative thoughts, it is much easier to become discouraged from whatever it is you want to do. Eliminate negative people from your life and start finding friends who have positive thoughts. This is much easier said than done, but once accomplished, you should see dramatic improvements in your levels of happiness and productivity. I can't tell you how many people in my life people have underestimated me, told me I couldn't do things, and where just overall worthless pieces of garbage. This is common to most everyone, whether you are a pro or a regular person. The best tool is to use this as motivation to reach your goals and prove those losers wrong. It is extremely satisfying to see the look on other peoples faces after you have just put on a peak performance that has dominated!

It is also a great idea to stay away from the newspapers and the news. It is extremely difficult to keep a positive frame of mind when you are filling your brain with all the horrible things that happened in the last day or week. I know you have probably heard this before... but actually do it! Try switching the news for reading motivational and inspiring books. Over the long term, you may be shocked at what such a simple change can do in your everyday life!

Also, be sure to catch any negative thoughts that you might be sending to yourself. One good way to do this is to write down your negative thoughts whenever they come to you. By writing them down and seeing them, you can have a better sense of how they are not true and how they will not help you. For example, if you find yourself thinking, "I'll never save any money," write that down and then tell yourself how it's not true. Another great strategy is to simply wear a rubber band on your wrist, and every time a negative thought pops in your head, snap it. This strategy has worked great for me and others I know as well. I would also highly recommend checking the great "Tapping" videos on YouTube. They can be very helpful. If you are serious about eliminating a negative thought pattern, then be sure to think about this negative thought while doing the exercise, and you will need to do this three times a day for two weeks to a month to really get stellar results.

A lot of times, negativity comes from fear. If you find yourself feeling anxious or afraid all of the time, it is critical that you eliminate this fear so that you can be feeling more positive and uplifting emotions on a regular basis. There is nothing more damaging to motivation then constantly running fears through your mind all day long. For more detailed information on how to overcome fear and anxiety, be sure to check out my books: Overcome Fear and Laughter and Humor Therapy.

Overcome Future Obstacles Now. As with any goal, you will usually run into an obstacle or two along the way. For example, if you're trying to stick to a diet and you go to a Christmas party, your obstacle will probably be all of the delicious-looking foods and desserts that people bring. If your goal is to get a promotion at work, an obstacle might be that you will have to get extra work done in less time or outperform an ambitious colleague. By thinking about what your future obstacles may be, you can strategize solutions to these problems before they even occur. It is much better to be prepared than to realize one day after many hours of work that you didn't anticipate a critical detail that is going to set you behind dramatically. Take your time to be smart, do your research, and the majority of the time you will come out smelling like roses.

Of course, you may run into an obstacle that you couldn't predict—if that happens, just stay positive and work through it. Maybe you are trying to save money but then your car engine fails. Unfortunately, you probably couldn't foresee that, especially if you have a newer car. Don't get discouraged. One good thing about obstacles is that they make you stronger. By trying to predict some of the more common obstacles associated with your goals, you will be less likely to get discouraged in the event of a roadblock.

Reward and Give Yourself Credit. While working to reach your goals, one great way to stay motivated is to reward and credit yourself for your progress.

Rewards are a great incentive and motivator because who doesn't love getting rewarded? If you're working toward a long-term goal and you reward yourself for every step you take toward it, don't reward yourself with the same thing every time—switch it up and you will be less likely to get bored. You can reward yourself with a vacation, a nice dinner, a full body massage, a trip to the movies, or anything else that you find appropriate.

Give yourself credit, too. If your goal is to put on five pounds of muscle in three months, check the scale at the end of each month and say, "I knew I could do it! Now I am much stronger and I will only get better!"

Prepare For Failure. This technique is a little similar to the technique about trying to predict your obstacles but it does have some unique aspects. As you probably know, sometimes you will not win. Sometimes you will not reach your goal or you won't reach it in the time frame that you wanted. To stop yourself from becoming discouraged, prepare for failure.

Prep yourself to look at failure in a positive light. If you try something and you fail, you may realize that you need to do something different. Don't view it as a complete loss—view it as a lesson learned. Tell yourself that you will not make the same mistakes in your next venture. If you start working toward a huge goal with high expectations just to find out that you won't be able to make it, you will most likely become very disappointed. While you shouldn't *not* reach for the stars, just keep in mind that you will use failure to your advantage if it does occur. Sometimes more important things pop up or life gets in the way. As you have already heard many times before, one of the great keys to success is to just never give up. Keep moving forward with dogged determination, despite and setbacks that may occur along the way and eventually you will get there.

Eliminate Excuses. Excuses are a big reason that many people fall into the groove of becoming unmotivated. When you continually make excuses for why you are not progressing toward your goals, you are not going to get anywhere. A good way to catch an excuse is when you hear yourself saying, "but." Whenever you hear or feel that word coming off your tongue, stop yourself and don't let it come out.

For example, if you hear yourself saying, "I really want to put this $20 away for the future but I also really want this new shirt…" immediately recognize that you're making an excuse for not sticking to your goal. Another good idea is to use reverse psychology on your excuses. For example, you could say, "I really want to buy that new shirt *but* if I do that, I won't reach my goal of saving."

View Your Most Important Tasks From a Different Angle. When it comes to reaching your goals, sometimes you have to prioritize your most important tasks to stay motivated—otherwise, you can get caught up in things that don't matter. Sometimes, you're most important tasks in reaching your goals can seem hard, boring, and annoying. Instead of looking at those tasks as "musts," look at them as "wants."

By doing them, you can get closer to what you want. Looking at your goals in this way is a great technique for staying motivated. Also, a great way to prioritize your most important tasks is to create a to-do list or keep a planner handy. When you're able to plan and organize your days, your chances of taking steps toward your goals gets better. When I am working at my desk, I like to cut up small pieces of white paper and put doing a goal that needs to be accomplished. I will then order those pieces of paper in the order of most importance and then throw them away when the task is complete.

Visualize Your Success. Visualization can be a very powerful technique for staying motivated. Think about what you want and why you want it. Then, think about what your life will be like once you've got it. For example, if you are struggling financially, think about what your life will be like once you've saved money—you can relax knowing that you're a little more financially secure or you won't have to spend so much money on public transportation because you'll have enough money to buy a car. Everything you visualize will be different based on your individual goals and your own self. Visualization is something that the top pros in the world do on a consistent basis. Be sure to make visualization a habit that you do every day to dramatically increase your chances of success. It is also a good idea to visualize a scene as if you were ten to fifteen feet away in the 3rd person. Just allow the scene to flow naturally with you doing everything perfectly to achieve the desired goal.

Chapter 4: Motivation Killers

Remember how I said in Chapter 3 that motivation doesn't just happen, you have to make it happen? Unfortunately, there are some common behaviors that *do* seem to automatically happen and they are huge motivation killers! Although it can be hard *not* to act or think in the ways that you are about to read about, it is important to keep this information in the back of your head. That way, next time you catch yourself acting or feeling a certain way, you can stop it before all of your motivations die down.

The Most Common Motivation Killers

Being Ungrateful. When you're ungrateful, it is easy to lose sight of the small things in life, which often become the most important things when they're suddenly taken away. Practicing gratitude can help you learn how to appreciate the things around you and in your life. Being grateful can help you stay motivated because it feels good, you know what your values are, and you can gain a better sense of your hard work. When you are halfway to reaching one of your goals, be grateful that you got that far and be grateful for what you've learned in the process. That way, you will want to go on and get the end results. Also, be sure to be grateful for all the other incredible things in your life. When you really stop to think about it, you may be surprised at all the incredible things we have to be grateful for in the modern age.

Jealousy. Jealously is a huge motivational killer because when you get wrapped up in it, you tend to get caught up on how you *don't* have something instead of spending that time trying to get it yourself. Most likely, you have friends who love to show things off in real life and on social media—sometimes seeing something on social media is the worst because you automatically think that someone else is living the perfect life while your not. Any time you are feeling jealous, don't let yourself get wrapped up in it—instead, think about what kind of goals you can set to get the things going that *you* want, and start to work on them. By knowing that you will be working toward getting something that you really want, your chances of achieving it will be much higher.

Impatience. You shouldn't confuse being impatient with having a sense of urgency, but if you are impatient, you will not likely get very far in life and towards your goals. When you're impatient, you tend to forget things or make more mistakes than if you had slowed down and paid more attention. Sometimes impatience can be hard to tackle. It's different for everybody but one really good technique is to take a lot of breaks. Breaks can help you slow down and refocus on whatever it is that you're working on. Another good idea to is think about the great results that you can end up with when you exert a little bit of patience. Being impatient can give you a very bad reputation if you are rushing through things, being sloppy, cutting corners, and delivering subpar results that could easily have been rectified by taking the time necessary to do the task properly.

Feeling Overwhelmed. Feeling overwhelmed can be a huge motivation killer, but the good news is that there are ways around it. When you are feeling overwhelmed, reevaluate your life and see what you can take away. Prioritize the most important things in your life and put anything that is less important on the back-burner. If you're working toward a really huge goal, work toward it in small steps—don't try to get everything done all at once. This can be really overwhelming. Another good idea for fending off the feeling of being overwhelmed is to try to organize better. Organize your goals, organize your life, organize your computer, organize your house, and organize anything that is making you feel overwhelmed or anxious. Write down a list on a piece of paper of what you want to get organized and then let that serve as your map. Getting organized can be very therapeutic and it can definitely save you time and energy in the long run.

Being Unhealthy. It almost seems like being in good health is important to accomplish anything—and that includes staying motivated. When you're not in the best physical and mental shape, staying motivated toward anything can be very hard. If you're constantly fatigued, it can be hard to stay energized. Without energy, it can be hard to work toward anything. You don't have to be a bodybuilder or a nutritionist to stay motivated. However, it is important to make sure that you are getting enough sleep, eating foods that are actually healthy, and exercising at least a little bit each day. Also, not only is being in good health important for staying motivated, it's also crucial for living a long and happy life. For more detailed information on being healthy and full of energy, be sure to check out my bestselling books: Ultimate Health and Ultimate Energy.

Fear. If you are afraid of something and you do not address your fear, chances are you will not confront it. Fear is when you spend half of your life writing a novel and then you just never send it out to publishers because you're afraid of rejection. The emotion of fear is strong and negative at the same time. It can hold you back from endless opportunities if you don't know how to manage it. A good way to manage fear is to first identify what it is, and then ask yourself how you can beat it. By being aware of your fears, your chances of overcoming them are often better. To really learn how to blast your fears into oblivion, check out my book: Overcome Fear.

No Support. When you are alone in an endeavor, it tends to be much harder to accomplish things. If your friends, family, and loved ones do not agree with your goals, their chances of discouraging you tend to be much higher. However, even if your family and friends don't support you, you can still overcome this obstacle. Whenever you have the chance, take some time and connect with like-minded people. For example, if you're a writer trying to make it big, go online and find somebody with a similar goal. By building up your network of support, you can feel much more motivated. Also, when you stick to your efforts, you can experience great personal fulfillment. Remember, whatever you are doing is for yourself, not for anybody else. Don't forget to be your own support! Some of the greatest things in history have been accomplished by people who ignored their friends, family, teachers, and everyone else to follow their passion and make their dreams a reality.

Being Vague. If you are vague in your goals or your future plans, it can be hard to stay motivated. By being vague with yourself, you will not have a clear picture on what you really want. To help keep your motivation up, be specific in your goals, actions, and wants. This way, you will have a better idea of how to work toward them. Visualizing your goals can help you feel what it will be like to get the end results.

Chapter 5: Motivation Role Models

Throughout history, many people in various industries have served as motivational role models for future generations. These figures are people who have utilized motivation effectively to get the fame and authority that they have today as actors, life coaches, authors, inventors, musicians, and more. In this chapter, I will share the stories of some of the people who I believe have used motivation to get where they are today. These people have also spread the message of motivation to others. I hope that they are able to positively influence you and your outlook on life.

Motivational Role Models

Arnold Schwarzenegger. Arnold Schwarzenegger is probably my favorite role model and one of the reasons I got into serious bodybuilding. If you have never seen the movie "Pumping Iron", be sure to check it out. When you create something truly magical, it stands the test of time. That also stands true for the original movie "Conan The Barbarian" another incredible movie with one of the best soundtracks of all time. If you ever feel down and out, watch either of these movies to boost your motivation!

Arnold is now a very famous man, best known for his career in bodybuilding, acting, and his most recent career as the governor of California. Originally born in Austria, Arnold had a rough childhood. His father was an alcoholic and regularly put a damper on his dreams of being a bodybuilder. Determined to do what he wanted anyway, Arnold joined the army and snuck out to enter bodybuilding contests. When they caught him, they punished him, but after learning that he had won the contest, they actually began to support him. Arnold then came to America, won five Mr. Olympia Bodybuilding contests in a row and then starred in the documentary we talked about earlier, Pumping Iron, on his way to a historic 6th Mr. Olympia Title. After starring in some of the greatest action films of his era over several decades, Arnold felt inspired to get into politics because of his new-found life in America. He wanted to give back for all of the great opportunities he was given. All of Arnold's experience in life has enabled him to inspire others to do the same. Check out this YouTube video Who Do You Want To Be In Life? posted by Steven Toozer to hear one of his amazing motivational speeches. One of the main reasons people like Arnold is because they know that he is giving it his all. He is trying as hard as he can to succeed, and people can respect that.

Tony Robbins. Tony Robins is a life coach who is best known for helping people overcome fears, feel inspired, get into the best health, and make the most out of their lives. Starting off as a seminar promoter, Tony soon got into the career of a self-help life coach, creating a series of audio-tapes that reached millions of people around the world. My favorite being the "Get The Edge" series, which I've listened to many times. He runs the Leadership Academy, where people can learn to find themselves by overcoming their personal challenges. He also works with students and prisoners, helping them learn how to improve the quality of life for others. Tony Robbins is a great example of a person who is motivated by intrinsic factors. He has held many seminars and workshops and has inspired millions of people. He is truly one of a kind. To see him in action, please check out this YouTube video posted by the Affirmation Institute: Words of Wisdom: Tony Robbins' Compilation. I hope it leaves you feeling as motivated and inspired as it did me. With a new worth of over 480 million dollars, Tony could easily retire. But he continues to press onward, helping hundreds of thousands of people a year and continuing to try and find better ways to do things and be successful. Like Arnold, Tony's strong work ethic and intelligence is what makes him highly respected throughout the world.

Thomas Edison. Thomas Edison is most famous for being the inventor of the light bulb. However, many people are unaware that he failed at least 1,000 times before he was finally successful. Although the exact number of times he failed is unclear, he is most famous for saying that he never actually failed—he just found 1,000 ways that didn't work. Thomas Edison is a great example of how motivation and persistence can result in something great—in this case, the light bulb, something that you use every day. Another example of someone who is able to get motivated and stay motivated over long periods of time to achieve truly incredible things.

Lance Armstrong. Lance Armstrong is a famous cyclist and athlete who was at the top of his career in 1996. However, he was then diagnosed with testicular cancer, which quickly spread to his lungs. It was so severe that doctors only said he had a 50% chance of living. Lance was persistent in receiving chemotherapy and surgery and he maintained a great attitude throughout the whole process. Amazingly, he beat the cancer and returned to cycling, where he eventually won the Tour De France and then held first place for seven years. Lance's motivational story comes with the message to never give up, no matter how bad your life gets.

Eminem. Marshall Mathers, better known as famous rapper Eminem, is a very motivational role model in the music industry. He grew up in a broken household, abandoned by his father and raised by a young mother. They lived in Detroit, where they were the minority. Eminem was bullied so badly in school that he was once put into a coma by one of the beatings. He dropped out of high school and got into rapping with some friends. After much effort and determination, he was recruited and got a record deal.

Despite many legal and drug issues, he worked hard on his rap career to give his daughter, Hailey, a better childhood than he had. One of his latest albums is centered on his recovery process. Eminem is a great example of somebody who rose to fame from nothing, who pursued to make a better life for his family because he was motivated by his daughter, and who has overcome many personal challenges. Despite all of his troubles and woes, he never stopped making music.

To see Eminem's thoughts on motivation, check out this YouTube video posted by the Vevo Channel: Eminem (who am I) Motivation Documentary 2013.

Bethany Hamilton. When Bethany Hamilton was 13, she was attacked by a shark while surfing and lost her entire left arm. After her recovery, she was determined to get back on her surfboard. She did not let the trauma of the event or the fact that she was disabled stop her. She was back in the water less than a month after her accident. Using a special surfboard, she taught herself to swim and surf with one arm. She went on to win major competitions. Bethany Hamilton is a great motivational role model because she did not let a huge, traumatic event stop her from doing what she loves. While many people would be too afraid to go back in the water, she was back in it weeks later. To hear Bethany's thoughts on the purpose of life, check out this YouTube video, Bethany Hamilton On Life's Purpose by Positively Positive.

Maya Angelou. Maya Angelou, an American poet and author who recently passed away, but left behind a huge legacy of motivation. Best known for her number of written works, she pursued a PhD degree and represented the African American culture after overcoming a traumatic childhood. Maya was a well-known public speaker who often encouraged people to treat others kindly, adding that people will forget what you've said to them but they will never forget if you've made them feel bad. Many of her works have been used to educate others on topics such as race and self-esteem. She has not only been a motivational figure to African Americans but to many people around the world.

Motivational YouTube Videos

Here are some of my favorite YouTube Inspirational and Motivational Videos. Feel free to make them part of your daily ritual for motivation success.

How Great I Am by mbm34

Six Secrets To Success posted by Travis Fisher

I am a Champion posted by Pawel Jedrzejak

Dare To Be Great by Safin de Zane

The Difference Between A Winner And A Loser posted by Refpeople – Social Network

Never Quit - Motivational Video by MotivationGrid

Quiet Desperation Motivational Video by Kevin Tylecote

Be Fearless posted by hummerchriss

It's Possible posted by Mind Innovation

Chapter 6: Motivational Quotes

At times, it can be hard to feel motivated. Life can be very challenging and full of setbacks and it can be easy to give up. However, never give up! This chapter aims to provide some of the most motivational quotes ever to help you stay on track. Anytime you are in need of an inspirational boost, refer to this chapter. Write out your favorite quotes, hang them in your workspace, keep them in your wallet, or do whatever you need to effectively utilize them. Just remember that hard works does indeed payoff and that with a great commitment and sacrifice come mighty rewards!

Motivational Quotes To Keep You Going

"Give me a stock clerk with a goal and I'll give you a man who will make history. Give me a man with no goals and I'll give you a stock clerk" – James Cash Penny

"The state of your life is nothing more than a reflection of your state of mind" – Wayne Dyer

"Fix your eyes on perfection and you make almost everything speed towards it" – William Ellery Channing

"If you take responsibility for yourself you will develop a hunger to accomplish your dreams" – Les Brown

"What distinguishes us one from another is our dreams...and what we do to make them come about" – Joseph Epstein

"If you do what you've always done, you'll get what you've always gotten" – Anthony Robbins

"Every great human achievement is preceded by extended periods of dedicated, concentrated effort" – Brain Tracy

"The world of achievement has always belonged to the optimist" – J. Harold Wilkins

"If you have built castles in the air, your work need not be lost; that is where they should be. Now put the foundations under them" – Henry David Thoreau

"Success is never final and failure never fatal. It's courage that counts" – George F. Tiltonood

"The key is not to prioritize what's on your schedule, but to schedule your priorities" – Stephen R. Covey

"Don't let anyone tell you that you can't do it. You can. It's up to you. Decide to do it and follow through" – Porter Freeman

"I've always made a total effort, even when the odds seemed entirely against me. I never quit trying; I never felt that I didn't have a chance to win" – Arnold Palmer

"A great pleasure in life is doing what people say you cannot do" – Walter Bagehot

"When you cannot make up your mind which of two evenly balanced courses of action you should take, choose the bolder" – W.J. Slim

"If you don't quit, and don't cheat, and don't run home when trouble arrives, you can only win" – Shelley Long

"If you don't risk anything, you risk even more" – Erica Jong

"Questions focus our thinking. Ask empowering questions like, what's good about this? What's not perfect about it yet? What am I going to do next time? How can I do this and have fun doing it?" - Charles Connolly

"A problem is a chance to do your best" – Duke Ellington

"Mistakes are merely steps up the ladder" – Paul J. Meyer

"Remember: if you're not experiencing failure, you're not working hard enough" – Jeffery J. Mayer

"He that is good with a hammer tends to think everything is a nail" – Abraham Maslow

"If passion drives you, let reason hold the reigns" – Benjamin Franklin

"Luck is what happens when preparation meets opportunity" – Elmer Letterman

"Men may doubt what you say, but they will believe what you do" – Lewis Cass

Conclusion

I hope this book was able to help you to learn how to harness the power of **Motivation** to take yourself to the most amazing places in life.

The next step is to figure out where you want to start first. If you followed along and wrote out your goals, refer to your list and pick a goal to start with. If not, write out your goals and focus on the most important one. Ask yourself why that goal is important to you. Then eliminate any motivation killers that are present in your life and go achieve it! If at any time you feel discouraged, go back to Chapter 5 and 6 and reread your favorite motivational quote or watch your favorite video.

Finally, if you discovered at least one thing that has helped you or that you think would be beneficial to someone else, be sure to take a few seconds to easily post a quick positive review. As an author, your positive feedback is desperately needed. Your highly valuable five star reviews are like a river of golden joy flowing through a sunny forest of mighty trees and beautiful flowers! *To do your good deed in making the world a better place by helping others with your valuable insight, just leave a nice review.*

My Other Books and Audio Books
www.AcesEbooks.com

Peak Performance Books

Health Books

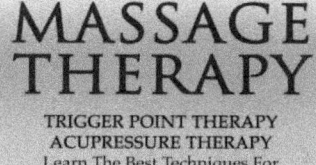

Be sure to check out my audio books as well!

 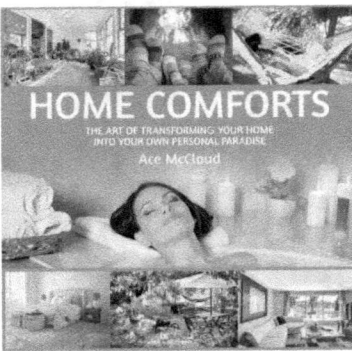 

Check out my website at: **www.AcesEbooks.com** for a complete list of all of my books and high quality audio books. I enjoy bringing you the best knowledge in the world and wish you the best in using this information to make your journey through life better and more enjoyable! **Best of luck to you!**

www.ingramcontent.com/pod-product-compliance
Lightning Source LLC
Chambersburg PA
CBHW051430070526
44584CB00023B/3666